HELLO PRAYER WARRIOR!

I am so excited for you, friend! You won't be surprised to hear this, but I am super passionate about prayer. And I don't mean this as a ritual or just a calming experience, but as a conversation with our Father in heaven. If you have been a Christian for long though, this little fact can get lost on us. The reality that we can connect with God on an intimate level every day without bounds is truly amazing.

But here's the thing - our world is loud. It's distracting and it's fighting to keep us from that communion with God. So this journal was designed to be a practical tool that helps focus your heart. If you are hoping to change your prayer life, it won't change without (you guessed it!)... a change. :)

So, I'm challenging you to commit to 10 minutes of **quality** *prayer time* a day for the first month. Just 10 minutes. Every day. One Month. At the end of the month, journal what has changed:

> *1. in your relationship with God*
> *2. in your heart*
> *3. in your circumstances*

Return to this list when the world tries to distract you, because it inevitably will.

Remember friend, **prayer is worth the time you put into it.** I believe it's the greatest investment we can make in our marriages, kids, communities, businesses, friendships, everything.

I'm rooting for you. I'm praying for you, too. And we're just an email away (info@valmariepaper.com) if you need a pep talk!

Val

THIS JOURNAL BELONGS TO

_____

ACCOUNTABILITY AWAITS!

We're not just here to sell you a prayer journal. Val Marie Paper wants to help you really use it! We get emails and messages daily from people about how life-changing this format has been in their prayer lives and we want the same for you too!!

Here's how VMP wants to keep you motivated:

VIDEO TUTORIAL

We've got super practical tutorials on how to use each section of this journal. Go to valmariepaper.com/tutorial for access!

GRAB A FRIEND

Grab a friend who's also looking to deepen their prayer life and share your commitment to pray more and check in on eachother weekly to share prayer requests, obstacles, victories or to pray together!

PRAY CONFIDENTLY AND CONSISTENTLY BOOK

This book was written after thousands of conversations over the last 9 years, addressing the fifteen greatest weights holding back our prayer life. It covers so many challenges to our prayer lives while being accessible and practical. Available on Amazon and signed copies at valmariepaper.com.

ONLINE PRAYER COURSE

We've created a prayer course called *Developing a Fluency of Prayer* to help create a foundation for praying. The 9 modules cover basic truths on prayer, how to hear God more clearly, how to pray with others and for others, how to use Scripture in our prayer times, addressing obstacles and more. Bonus: You can go through as a small group for one flat price! Available at valmariepaper.com.

SOCIAL ENCOURAGEMENT

@ValMariePaper - For tips and hacks to use for your journal

VMP Society - This Facebook group is a place to interact with fellow believers on a mission to pray more. Ask questions and find tips and hacks from other journal users. Go to bit.ly/vmpsociety to join.

PRAYER IN A NOISY WORLD PODCAST

What if the noise in your earbuds could help you turn down the noise of the world? Our podcast was created do just that! You'll find interviews, how-to's and guided prayers on different topics related to prayer.

HOW TO USE YOUR JOURNAL

SET UP

1. Fill out sections *before* the month starts if you can. Once the month gets started, I'm less likely to use my journal in those small, quick moments where I can pray. If you can't fill out beforehand, fill out each section as you pray for them instead of all at once. If you miss a month completely, feel free to rip it out! Don't let blank pages discourage you.

2. Get creative! We've created prompts but know they may not fit your needs perfectly, so this is where you make the journal your own. Not married? In the "My Loves" section, list requests for your future spouse or even the mission that you devote your life to. Or have a section you wish was included? We've got a blank page with three sections to use as you wish! Examples: Small Group, Missionaries, Decision to Make, etc.

* Here are some examples of what you can include in each section. You can also flip the page to see a sample of a journal filled out!

ADORATION
+ a characteristic of God
+ names of God
+ a verse of adoration

MONTHLY CHALLENGE
+ no phone before prayer
+ read a book on prayer
+ pray with others
+ pray Scripture
+ daily prayer walk
+ 10 minutes of silence

SCRIPTURE & QUOTES
+ truth to meditate on
+ prayer-starters
+ words from current read

WORLD & NATION
+ operationworld.com
+ biggest news stories
+ kids' sponsorships

MY COMMUNITY
+ co-workers
+ first responders
+ neighbors

MY CHURCH
+ pastor and leaders
+ specific ministries
+ small group

MY LOVES
+ spouse
+ children
+ future spouse / kids

FAMILY
+ immediate + extended

SWEET FRIENDS
+ text / call for updates
+ pray for new or deeper friendships

SALVATION
+ their initials
+ eyes to see the lost
+ opportunities to share

THE HEAVY
+ those to forgive
+ burdens on your heart

PERSONAL
+ character pain points
+ events coming up
+ questions for God

BIG GOALS
+ yearly / monthly goals
+ action steps

BLANK SPACES
+ business or ministry
+ expand on other sections
+ friends trying to conceive

---

3. Make a commitment. Try thinking through these questions to help you get the most out of your journal:

• *What do I hope to accomplish with this journal?* Knowing the desired end result is going to help figure out the best way to use it.

• *What don't I understand about how the journal was intended to be used?* Watch the tutorials. Ask questions in the Facebook group. Or email us!

• *What are the points of usual breakdown?* Where do I normally stop using something and why? Make a plan of action before it happens.

• *Based on my lifestyle, personality, etc. how should I use this?* If a feature we have doesn't serve you, make the decision not to use it so you don't see it as failing. Use the space in a different way.

• *What's my rhythm or routine going to be?* Don't just set up your journal and expect to use it. You need a plan for it. Put it on your calendar or write the habits you want to develop with it on the inside cover of the journal.

• *What else do I need to add in here so that it's something I keep handy?* What are you already consistently referencing daily that you can put in here? We have some insert options in our shop at valmariepaper.com.

DAILY USE

4. Start with adoration and Scripture. Get fed on truth to help focus your mind, then flip to whichever section you'll cover that day.

5. Pray a section or two a day. Our vision is not that you'd pray through every page of the month every day! You'll get burnt out or feel overwhelmed.

6. Add to your answered prayers throughout the month so you don't forget them when you reach the end of the month! Those little circles at the beginning of each line are to check off any prayers that get answered that month. Not all requests are so black and white, but you can mark any requests you saw God work in.

7. Use the lined pages for anything you'd like to reflect on that month. You can write out a few long form prayers, gratitudes, verses of encouragement that relate to that months challenges, sermon notes, affirmations or whatever would be most helpful to have handy in your prayer journal. If you end up wanting more space to write prayers, check out our Signature Prayer Journal, designed with the same monthly prompts as well as 29 pages to write out prayers daily.

January

ADORATION

My REFUGE
God is our refuge and strength, an ever
present help in trouble. - Psalm 46:1

· Think on a quality of the Lord's to meditate on this month ·

SCRIPTURE

Trust in the Lord with all your heart, and do not
lean on your own understanding. In all your ways
acknowledge him, and he will make straight your
paths - Proverbs 3:5-6

Do not be conformed to this world, but be
transformed by the renewal of your mind, that by
testing you may discern what is the will
of God, what is good and acceptable and
perfect. - Romans 12:2

*"If you ABIDE IN ME, and My words abide in you, ask whatever
you wish, and IT WILL BE DONE for you. - John 15:7*

---

the CHALLENGE

Text Jamie weekly

· Write a goal that will help you make prayer a habit ·

our WORLD & NATION

○ Haiti and Hope for Kidz program
○ political leaders
○ racial reconciliation

· Lift up a country's biggest need, our nation, leaders and current events ·

my COMMUNITY

○ Neighbors - Stella, George
○ Bridge Ministry
○ _____

· Pray for needs in your neighborhood or city ·

my CHURCH

○ pastor, elders and staff
○ Church budget
○ Marriage Mentor program
○ SG - Karen surgery, Rachel new

· Pray for needs in your church, small group, etc. ·

---

my LOVES

○ Family - joy despite hard season, peace to
○   flood our home, no sickness, kindness
○ Tyler - work tension with foe, back pain,
○   leader in our house
○ Vivi - confidence in school work, sleep,
○   relationship with Vana
○ Vana - salvation, potty training, sleep,
○   relationship with Vivi
○ _____

· Lift up your spouse, kids, future spouse or biggest passion to the Lord ·

my FAMILY

○ Beth & Thomas - trying to conceive
○ Mindy & Shawn - job situation for both
○ Mom and Dad - selling house
○ Papp
○ Mawmaw & Pawpaw
○ _____
○ _____
○ _____
○ _____
○ _____

· Place in the Lord's hands those nearest to you ·

---

sweet FRIENDS

○ Carrie - pregnancy, 20 week ultrasound Jan 22
○ Ainsley - deciding school for Dallas
○ Terry - health answers
○ Jillian - marriage
○ Nancy - family tension
○ _____
○ _____
○ _____
○ _____
○ _____
○ _____
○ _____

· Bring before God things that your friends are facing ·

SALVATION

○ SB _____   _____ W ○
○ GD _____   _____ HR ○

· Pray for people in your life to come to know Christ ·

the HEAVY

○ Forgive Evelyn
○ _____

· Ask God to help you forgive hurts and love the hard to love ·

SAMPLE PAGES

PERSONAL

- ○ Joy in Christ
- ○ Peace in Christ
- ○ Deeper prayer life
- ○ Figure out health issues
- ○ Present with the girls
- ○ Discipline with food
- ○ _____
- ○ _____
- ○ _____
- ○ _____
- ○ _____
- ○ _____

Share with the Lord your current needs, trials and fears

big GOALS

- ○ Write 10,000 words in quarter 2
- ○ Get better at speaking
- ○ Pursue emotional health
- ○ Start lessons with girls
- ○ _____
- ○ _____
- ○ _____

· Invite God to be a part of your dreams for this month and beyond ·

Missionaries

- ○ Shoemakers in Haiti
- ○ Moses in Sierra Leone
- ○ Burundi
- ○ Cassie in Peru
- ○ _____
- ○ _____

Marriage

- ○ Finding quality time to talk
- ○ Better communication
- ○ Shine bright for the Lord
- ○ Love selflessly
- ○ Sharpen each other
- ○ _____

Val Marie Paper

- ○ Customers to experience the Lord in prayer
- ○ Team - work together well
- ○ Sales
- ○ Making good decisions on opportunities
- ○ Writing - be a vessel for the Lord
- ○ _____

· Write down everything else that concerns you ·

GOD ANSWERS

Now, our God, we give you thanks, and praise your glorious name. - 1 Chronicles 29:13

Mindy found a great job. Totally unexpected but perfect for her.
Seeing my prayer life change!
Got to share our faith as a couple with Jude and Sarah. Didn't expect to be a light as a couple in that way!

January

1. Prayer time with Mrs. Sharon
2. Quiet morning time
3. New fiction
4. Warm fire
5. Hot tea
6. Giggles with Vivi
7. Long chat with Tyler
8. Snuggling with Vana

_____
_____
_____

Jan 2, 2021

Father, thank you for your above and beyond gracious love for me. I will never stop marveling at the fact that you desire to spend time with me. Put a fire in my heart for you Lord. I am yours draw near to me God as I draw near to you. And may I never that true life only comes when I'm abiding in you. So many things are on my heart today. First, I want to thank you for the friendships you've given me. I confess that I've taken them for granted and I've judged others who do things differently than me, but I pray you'd give me fresh eyes to see my friends the way you see them. Show me how to love unconditionally and love them even in prayer. I pray for my friends Cathie, Ainsley, Terry and Jillian you know the requests on their heart. I especially lift up Nancy and the family tension that's left her feeling lonely and helpless Lord. Comfort her Lord like only you can and show me how I can be a friend in the middle of her heartache. I love you Lord. In Jesus' Name, amen

_____
_____
_____
_____

when you're
FEELING STUCK

ADORATION

Psalm 8, Revelation 4, Psalm 100, Psalm 104, Psalm 136, Psalm 139

QUESTIONS TO MEDITATE ON:

Who is God? What words describe Him?
What things make Him different from all other gods?
What makes Him different from any human?

CONFESSION

Proverbs 28:13, Psalm 51, Daniel 9, James 5:16, 1 John 1:5-10, Ezra 9

QUESTIONS TO GET YOU STARTED:

Where do I find myself pulling away from God?
What areas do I not want to bring to light?
What would I be embarrassed to admit to anyone?

THANKSGIVING

1 Thessalonians 5:18, Isaiah 12, Hebrews 13:15, Colossians 3

QUESTIONS TO GET YOU STARTED:

What can you show God gratitude for today?
What things do you typically take for granted?
What are the hidden blessings in the struggles?

SUPPLICATION

1 Timothy 2:1-4, Philippians 4, Luke 22:42, Psalm 37

QUESTIONS TO GET YOU STARTED:

What is happening around you that needs prayer?
What things can only God do in your situation?
Are you allowing God to shape your heart and desires?

ADORATION

· Think on a quality of the Lord's to meditate on this month ·

SCRIPTURE

Write a verse or verses that you want to meditate on or verses related to your requests this month that you can incorporate into your prayers.

the CHALLENGE

· Write a goal that will help you make prayer a habit ·

our WORLD & NATION

○ _____

○ _____

○ _____

· Lift up a country's biggest need, our nation, leaders and current events ·

my COMMUNITY

○ _____

○ _____

○ _____

· Pray for needs in your neighborhood or city ·

my CHURCH

○ _____

○ _____

○ _____

○ _____

○ _____

· Pray for needs in your church, small group, etc. ·

my LOVES

○ _____
○ _____
○ _____
○ _____
○ _____
○ _____
○ _____
○ _____
○ _____

· Lift up your spouse, kids, future spouse or biggest passion to the Lord ·

my FAMILY

○ _____
○ _____
○ _____
○ _____
○ _____
○ _____
○ _____
○ _____
○ _____
○ _____
○ _____

· Place in the Lord's hands those nearest to you ·

sweet F R I E N D S

○ _____

○ _____

○ _____

○ _____

○ _____

○ _____

○ _____

○ _____

○ _____

○ _____

○ _____

○ _____

○ _____

· Bring before God things that your friends are facing ·

S A L V A T I O N

○ _____   _____ ○

○ _____   _____ ○

· Pray for people in your life to come to know Christ ·

the H E A V Y

○ _____

○ _____

· Ask God to help you forgive hurts and love the hard to love ·

PERSONAL

○ _____
○ _____
○ _____
○ _____
○ _____
○ _____
○ _____
○ _____
○ _____
○ _____
○ _____
○ _____

· Share with the Lord your current needs, trials and fears ·

big GOALS

○ _____
○ _____
○ _____
○ _____
○ _____
○ _____
○ _____
○ _____

· Invite God to be a part of your dreams for this month and beyond ·

_____

○ _____
○ _____
○ _____
○ _____
○ _____
○ _____

_____

○ _____
○ _____
○ _____
○ _____
○ _____
○ _____

_____

○ _____
○ _____
○ _____
○ _____
○ _____
○ _____

· Write down everything else that concerns you ·

GOD ANSWERS

Now, our God, we give you thanks, and praise
your glorious name. - 1 Chronicles 29:13

_____

_____

_____

_____

_____

_____

_____

_____

_____

_____

_____

_____

_____

_____

_____

_____

_____

_____

_____

_____

_____

_____

_____

_____

This is where things get really good. It's time to count the fruit. Praise
the Lord for this month's answered prayers. And those requests that
weren't answered how you hoped? Write those down too and surrender
them to the Lord in faith that He knows exactly what He's doing.

_____

ADORATION

_____

_____

_____

· Think on a quality of the Lord's to meditate on this month ·

SCRIPTURE

_____

_____

_____

_____

_____

_____

_____

_____

_____

_____

_____

_____

Write a verse or verses that you want to meditate on or verses related to your requests this month that you can incorporate into your prayers.

the CHALLENGE

· Write a goal that will help you make prayer a habit ·

our WORLD & NATION

○ _____
○ _____
○ _____

· Lift up a country's biggest need, our nation, leaders and current events ·

my COMMUNITY

○ _____
○ _____
○ _____

· Pray for needs in your neighborhood or city ·

my CHURCH

○ _____
○ _____
○ _____
○ _____
○ _____

· Pray for needs in your church, small group, etc. ·

my LOVES

○ _____
○ _____
○ _____
○ _____
○ _____
○ _____
○ _____
○ _____
○ _____

· Lift up your spouse, kids, future spouse or biggest passion to the Lord ·

my FAMILY

○ _____
○ _____
○ _____
○ _____
○ _____
○ _____
○ _____
○ _____
○ _____
○ _____
○ _____

· Place in the Lord's hands those nearest to you ·

sweet FRIENDS

○ _____
○ _____
○ _____
○ _____
○ _____
○ _____
○ _____
○ _____
○ _____
○ _____
○ _____
○ _____
○ _____

· Bring before God things that your friends are facing ·

SALVATION

○ _____   _____ ○
○ _____   _____ ○

· Pray for people in your life to come to know Christ ·

the HEAVY

○ _____
○ _____

· Ask God to help you forgive hurts and love the hard to love ·

PERSONAL

○ ———————————————————————
○ ———————————————————————
○ ———————————————————————
○ ———————————————————————
○ ———————————————————————
○ ———————————————————————
○ ———————————————————————
○ ———————————————————————
○ ———————————————————————
○ ———————————————————————
○ ———————————————————————
○ ———————————————————————

· Share with the Lord your current needs, trials and fears ·

big GOALS

○ ———————————————————————
○ ———————————————————————
○ ———————————————————————
○ ———————————————————————
○ ———————————————————————
○ ———————————————————————
○ ———————————————————————
○ ———————————————————————

· Invite God to be a part of your dreams for this month and beyond ·

_____

○ _____
○ _____
○ _____
○ _____
○ _____
○ _____

_____

○ _____
○ _____
○ _____
○ _____
○ _____
○ _____

_____

○ _____
○ _____
○ _____
○ _____
○ _____
○ _____

· Write down everything else that concerns you ·

GOD ANSWERS

Now, our God, we give you thanks, and praise
your glorious name. - 1 Chronicles 29:13

_____

_____

_____

_____

_____

_____

_____

_____

_____

_____

_____

_____

_____

_____

_____

_____

_____

_____

_____

_____

_____

_____

_____

This is where things get really good. It's time to count the fruit. Praise
the Lord for this month's answered prayers. And those requests that
weren't answered how you hoped? Write those down too and surrender
them to the Lord in faith that He knows exactly what He's doing.

_____

ADORATION

_____
_____
_____

· Think on a quality of the Lord's to meditate on this month ·

SCRIPTURE

_____
_____
_____
_____
_____
_____
_____
_____
_____
_____
_____
_____

Write a verse or verses that you want to meditate on or verses related to your requests this month that you can incorporate into your prayers.

the CHALLENGE

· Write a goal that will help you make prayer a habit ·

our WORLD & NATION

○ _____
○ _____
○ _____

· Lift up a country's biggest need, our nation, leaders and current events ·

my COMMUNITY

○ _____
○ _____
○ _____

· Pray for needs in your neighborhood or city ·

my CHURCH

○ _____
○ _____
○ _____
○ _____
○ _____

· Pray for needs in your church, small group, etc. ·

my LOVES

○ _____

○ _____

○ _____

○ _____

○ _____

○ _____

○ _____

○ _____

○ _____

· Lift up your spouse, kids, future spouse or biggest passion to the Lord ·

my FAMILY

○ _____

○ _____

○ _____

○ _____

○ _____

○ _____

○ _____

○ _____

○ _____

○ _____

○ _____

· Place in the Lord's hands those nearest to you ·

sweet FRIENDS

○ _____
○ _____
○ _____
○ _____
○ _____
○ _____
○ _____
○ _____
○ _____
○ _____
○ _____
○ _____
○ _____

· Bring before God things that your friends are facing ·

SALVATION

○ _____   _____ ○
○ _____   _____ ○

· Pray for people in your life to come to know Christ ·

the HEAVY

○ _____
○ _____

· Ask God to help you forgive hurts and love the hard to love ·

PERSONAL

○ _____

○ _____

○ _____

○ _____

○ _____

○ _____

○ _____

○ _____

○ _____

○ _____

○ _____

○ _____

· Share with the Lord your current needs, trials and fears ·

big GOALS

○ _____

○ _____

○ _____

○ _____

○ _____

○ _____

○ _____

○ _____

· Invite God to be a part of your dreams for this month and beyond ·

_____

○ _____
○ _____
○ _____
○ _____
○ _____
○ _____

_____

○ _____
○ _____
○ _____
○ _____
○ _____
○ _____

_____

○ _____
○ _____
○ _____
○ _____
○ _____
○ _____

· Write down everything else that concerns you ·

GOD ANSWERS

Now, our God, we give you thanks, and praise
your glorious name. - 1 Chronicles 29:13

_____

_____

_____

_____

_____

_____

_____

_____

_____

_____

_____

_____

_____

_____

_____

_____

_____

_____

_____

_____

_____

_____

_____

_____

_____

_____

This is where things get really good. It's time to count the fruit. Praise
the Lord for this month's answered prayers. And those requests that
weren't answered how you hoped? Write those down too and surrender
them to the Lord in faith that He knows exactly what He's doing.

_____

ADORATION

_____
_____
_____

· Think on a quality of the Lord's to meditate on this month ·

SCRIPTURE

_____
_____
_____
_____
_____
_____
_____
_____
_____
_____
_____
_____
_____

Write a verse or verses that you want to meditate on or verses related to your
requests this month that you can incorporate into your prayers.

the CHALLENGE

· Write a goal that will help you make prayer a habit ·

our WORLD & NATION

○ _____

○ _____

○ _____

· Lift up a country's biggest need, our nation, leaders and current events ·

my COMMUNITY

○ _____

○ _____

○ _____

· Pray for needs in your neighborhood or city ·

my CHURCH

○ _____

○ _____

○ _____

○ _____

○ _____

· Pray for needs in your church, small group, etc. ·

my LOVES

○ _____
○ _____
○ _____
○ _____
○ _____
○ _____
○ _____
○ _____
○ _____

· Lift up your spouse, kids, future spouse or biggest passion to the Lord ·

my FAMILY

○ _____
○ _____
○ _____
○ _____
○ _____
○ _____
○ _____
○ _____
○ _____
○ _____
○ _____

· Place in the Lord's hands those nearest to you ·

sweet FRIENDS

○ _____

○ _____

○ _____

○ _____

○ _____

○ _____

○ _____

○ _____

○ _____

○ _____

○ _____

○ _____

○ _____

· Bring before God things that your friends are facing ·

SALVATION

○ _____   _____ ○

○ _____   _____ ○

· Pray for people in your life to come to know Christ ·

the HEAVY

○ _____

○ _____

· Ask God to help you forgive hurts and love the hard to love ·

PERSONAL

- ○ _____
- ○ _____
- ○ _____
- ○ _____
- ○ _____
- ○ _____
- ○ _____
- ○ _____
- ○ _____
- ○ _____
- ○ _____
- ○ _____

· Share with the Lord your current needs, trials and fears ·

big GOALS

- ○ _____
- ○ _____
- ○ _____
- ○ _____
- ○ _____
- ○ _____
- ○ _____
- ○ _____

· Invite God to be a part of your dreams for this month and beyond ·

_____

○ _____
○ _____
○ _____
○ _____
○ _____
○ _____

_____

○ _____
○ _____
○ _____
○ _____
○ _____
○ _____

_____

○ _____
○ _____
○ _____
○ _____
○ _____
○ _____

· Write down everything else that concerns you ·

GOD ANSWERS

Now, our God, we give you thanks, and praise
your glorious name. - 1 Chronicles 29:13

_____

_____

_____

_____

_____

_____

_____

_____

_____

_____

_____

_____

_____

_____

_____

_____

_____

_____

_____

_____

_____

_____

_____

_____

This is where things get really good. It's time to count the fruit. Praise
the Lord for this month's answered prayers. And those requests that
weren't answered how you hoped? Write those down too and surrender
them to the Lord in faith that He knows exactly what He's doing.

ADORATION

_____

_____

_____

· Think on a quality of the Lord's to meditate on this month ·

SCRIPTURE

_____

_____

_____

_____

_____

_____

_____

_____

_____

_____

_____

_____

Write a verse or verses that you want to meditate on or verses related to your requests this month that you can incorporate into your prayers.

the CHALLENGE

· Write a goal that will help you make prayer a habit ·

our WORLD & NATION

○ _____

○ _____

○ _____

· Lift up a country's biggest need, our nation, leaders and current events ·

my COMMUNITY

○ _____

○ _____

○ _____

· Pray for needs in your neighborhood or city ·

my CHURCH

○ _____

○ _____

○ _____

○ _____

○ _____

· Pray for needs in your church, small group, etc. ·

my LOVES

○ _____

○ _____

○ _____

○ _____

○ _____

○ _____

○ _____

○ _____

○ _____

· Lift up your spouse, kids, future spouse or biggest passion to the Lord ·

my FAMILY

○ _____

○ _____

○ _____

○ _____

○ _____

○ _____

○ _____

○ _____

○ _____

○ _____

○ _____

· Place in the Lord's hands those nearest to you ·

sweet FRIENDS

○ _____
○ _____
○ _____
○ _____
○ _____
○ _____
○ _____
○ _____
○ _____
○ _____
○ _____
○ _____
○ _____

· Bring before God things that your friends are facing ·

SALVATION

○ _____   _____ ○
○ _____   _____ ○

· Pray for people in your life to come to know Christ ·

the HEAVY

○ _____
○ _____

· Ask God to help you forgive hurts and love the hard to love ·

PERSONAL

- ○ _____
- ○ _____
- ○ _____
- ○ _____
- ○ _____
- ○ _____
- ○ _____
- ○ _____
- ○ _____
- ○ _____
- ○ _____
- ○ _____

· Share with the Lord your current needs, trials and fears ·

big GOALS

- ○ _____
- ○ _____
- ○ _____
- ○ _____
- ○ _____
- ○ _____
- ○ _____
- ○ _____

· Invite God to be a part of your dreams for this month and beyond ·

_____

○ _____
○ _____
○ _____
○ _____
○ _____
○ _____

_____

○ _____
○ _____
○ _____
○ _____
○ _____
○ _____

_____

○ _____
○ _____
○ _____
○ _____
○ _____
○ _____

· *Write down everything else that concerns you* ·

GOD ANSWERS

Now, our God, we give you thanks, and praise
your glorious name. - 1 Chronicles 29:13

This is where things get really good. It's time to count the fruit. Praise
the Lord for this month's answered prayers. And those requests that
weren't answered how you hoped? Write those down too and surrender
them to the Lord in faith that He knows exactly what He's doing.

_____

ADORATION

_____

_____

_____

· Think on a quality of the Lord's to meditate on this month ·

SCRIPTURE

_____

_____

_____

_____

_____

_____

_____

_____

_____

_____

_____

_____

Write a verse or verses that you want to meditate on or verses related to your
requests this month that you can incorporate into your prayers.

the CHALLENGE

· Write a goal that will help you make prayer a habit ·

our WORLD & NATION

○ _____

○ _____

○ _____

· Lift up a country's biggest need, our nation, leaders and current events ·

my COMMUNITY

○ _____

○ _____

○ _____

· Pray for needs in your neighborhood or city ·

my CHURCH

○ _____

○ _____

○ _____

○ _____

○ _____

· Pray for needs in your church, small group, etc. ·

my LOVES

- _____
- _____
- _____
- _____
- _____
- _____
- _____
- _____
- _____

· Lift up your spouse, kids, future spouse or biggest passion to the Lord ·

my FAMILY

- _____
- _____
- _____
- _____
- _____
- _____
- _____
- _____
- _____
- _____
- _____

· Place in the Lord's hands those nearest to you ·

sweet FRIENDS

○ _____
○ _____
○ _____
○ _____
○ _____
○ _____
○ _____
○ _____
○ _____
○ _____
○ _____
○ _____
○ _____

· Bring before God things that your friends are facing ·

SALVATION

○ _____   _____ ○
○ _____   _____ ○

· Pray for people in your life to come to know Christ ·

the HEAVY

○ _____
○ _____

· Ask God to help you forgive hurts and love the hard to love ·

PERSONAL

○ _____
○ _____
○ _____
○ _____
○ _____
○ _____
○ _____
○ _____
○ _____
○ _____
○ _____
○ _____

· Share with the Lord your current needs, trials and fears ·

big GOALS

○ _____
○ _____
○ _____
○ _____
○ _____
○ _____
○ _____
○ _____

· Invite God to be a part of your dreams for this month and beyond ·

_____

○ _____
○ _____
○ _____
○ _____
○ _____
○ _____

_____

○ _____
○ _____
○ _____
○ _____
○ _____
○ _____

_____

○ _____
○ _____
○ _____
○ _____
○ _____
○ _____

· *Write down everything else that concerns you* ·

GOD ANSWERS

Now, our God, we give you thanks, and praise
your glorious name. - 1 Chronicles 29:13

_____

_____

_____

_____

_____

_____

_____

_____

_____

_____

_____

_____

_____

_____

_____

_____

_____

_____

_____

_____

_____

This is where things get really good. It's time to count the fruit. Praise
the Lord for this month's answered prayers. And those requests that
weren't answered how you hoped? Write those down too and surrender
them to the Lord in faith that He knows exactly what He's doing.

MORE FROM VMP

JOURNALS

Check out the Val Marie Paper shop for more products designed to encourage you in your faith walk including devotionals, prayer journals specifically for women, men, kids, teens, pregnancy and adoption.

BOOKS

Pray Confidently and Consistently: Finally Let Go of the Things Holding You Back From Your Most Important Conversation. Identify the weights burdening your prayer life and learn how to release them so you can go from a distant and dull prayer life to a vibrant and intimate one.

Springboard Prayers. A book of 125 written prayers for different circumstances, emotions, people, etc. Grab it from our shop today!

Visit our website to find free resources and products to promote a vibrant prayer life.

Made in the USA
Columbia, SC
18 December 2024

d025167a-ae86-49b8-b825-d80b04118edfR01